HER III

HER III

Pierre Alex Jeanty

Andrews McMeel
PUBLISHING®

If this book ever sounds like it's telling women how to be women, I beg you to examine it more deeply. I challenge you to look over the words with more care.

As I've stated in the beginning of every part of this series, I don't claim to be a great poet but a great observer.

I am simply an observer communicating what I've observed. The purpose of the books in this series has always been to speak to my fellow men about HER and highlight the things she needs him to know, hear, see, communicate, and understand in the simplest way. To also drop hints of empowerment for any woman reading it. Over the years, it became a much needed read for many women as they feel heard, understood, supported, and empowered.

The thing to never forget about HER is that she is in a constant stage of flowing from caterpillar to butterfly, shedding in different seasons in the name of growth. Who she is tomorrow will not always be who she is today, and yesterday's version of her has long faded.

If you ever wonder why this form of reincarnation is a must for her, remind yourself that growth doesn't come without change, and life itself doesn't happen without changes.

Dear,

Here's to standing on your own truth,
here's to finally reaching the point where
you wholeheartedly believe in yourself.
Here's to freeing yourself enough,
to caring for yourself enough,
to being enough.

Here's to all that you've become,
all that you've endured,
all that you've learned and applied.

Cheers to the new you.
You deserve to be celebrated.

The woman who was once prey to blood
thirsty wolves is now the tigress they are
afraid of meeting face-to-face.

Despite how they sank their teeth into her
heart and attempted to rip love out of it,
still she stands,
still she evolves,
still she becomes everything a strong
woman defines.

It's not that love kept changing faces,
it's that the faces you kept meeting were
empty of love and wore masks to hide it.
Love always looks the same;
so does the absence of it.

She'll compromise for love,
but she will not compromise to be loved
anymore.

You cannot swim your way back into her
heart after leaving her to scan the ocean for
a fish that was supposed to be better than
her.

When you let a good catch go,
you must also remember that it may never
swim back to you.

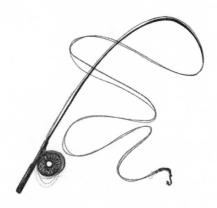

They left because they thought you would
never leave.
They dropped your heart because they
knew theirs was in safe hands.
They knew you wanted love more than you
wanted anything else.
The unfortunate truth is that they figured
out you don't quit too easily or give up on
love without enduring enough.
Show them it doesn't take much when love
can't find its way back to the relationship.

She will not call sand sugar,
nor will she mistake oil for water.
She may have been the girl who can be
blindly misled because of her hunger to
see better in people, but she's far removed
from that.
Your true colors will become the only
painting of you she sees.

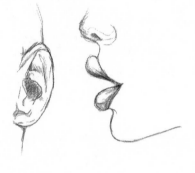

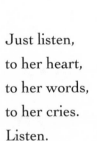

Just listen,
to her heart,
to her words,
to her cries.
Listen.
Listening to her will always be one of
the quickest routes to show that you care
deeply for her.

Bad timing shouldn't be a nickname for a relationship that has no good seed in it.

If he's chasing better,
let him go find it;
always remember that decision alone is
making room for your better to come.

What doesn't stay
only makes room for its replacement.

The curve of her smile was
the bowl that carried the tears.
Behind her calm laughs hid the
sadness that tried to swallow her.

She's learned to keep her own heart lit,
to feed her own flame,
and brush off what turned into ashes.
No one will make her cold again.

Dear,

Let me remind you that "your person" will never give you reasons to forget the person you are.

Don't you ever lose yourself for love once
again, my dear,
not for love, not for relationships, not for
friendship, not for anything.
Your identity never belonged in those
things; it never had to do with those things
in the first place but in who God made you
to be.

Acknowledge her thoughts.
Open your ears to her truth.
Make space for her to be heard.

Good women are not defined by their willingness to endure bad relationships and stay loyal to men who finally came to their senses.

Good women ought to be women who found the good in themselves, and know how to pull everything good out of them and share it with the world.

There's enough good women who will not give a man a chance to win her only to leave and later find out she was good.

There are men looking for love
and men looking to be loved.
One will reciprocate, while the other
resembles a well that you can only cast
wishes into and nothing more.

You took her heart,
ruined her trust, and
tainted her views on love.
I am not saying that you are fully
responsible,
because she must learn to get up on her
own strength,
but her knees are weak because of you.
Not because you swept her off her feet
but because you pushed her to fall into
the worst kinds of things.

She's not acting brand new.
She *is* brand new.
The internal work she has done turned
those lessons into seeds that drank her
tears and gave her stronger roots.

She is not the old dying rose you left.
She has turned a new leaf,
a better soul,
a stronger human being,
a wiser woman, and the flower that
bloomed through the drought.

Some men don't understand strength or see it because they are thirsty for weakness, hunters whose eyes search for prey.

To know her is to watch the sun steal the
sky for its morning show,
admire its beauty,
allow it to feed your skin while its breath
pulls drops of sweat from your pores.

It is also to watch the moon settle in the
darkness and illuminate the skies after the
sun performs its magic elsewhere.

Her asking to be treated with decency and
respect shouldn't be too much to ask or a
burden to give.
Especially when it's being requested from
those who want to hold her heart.
It should be the standard.

There's being a nice girl and being a
respectful woman.
The nice girl who used to be a doormat
that kissed the feet of men who had no
intention of truly loving her is gone.
In the same body, now lives a respectful
woman who will quickly set boundaries
and standards the nice girl was afraid to.
She's still nice, but she's not pushover nice.

A man with every intent to love you may encourage you not to be moved by your feelings, but he will never dismiss what you feel and help you process those feelings.

Dear,

It's not a crime to communicate how you
feel, neither is it a crime to have feelings
that they will not agree with.
Don't let them dismiss or redirect your
feelings, nor let them become your source
of validation.

She knows her voice and this is why she will not listen to anyone who makes her feel unheard.

Before you ask her what she will bring to
the table, it's best to make sure it's sturdy.

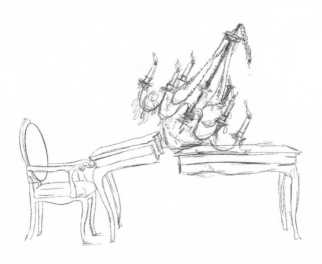

She will no longer be a home for lost men.

Creating a safe space for her to comfortably
pour herself, strip her soul naked—for you
to weaponize it and carefully craft your
manipulation is terrible.
How can you listen to her story and choose
the best way to be a villain?

Stay far away from the men who feel that
they only need a woman for cooking,
cleaning, and sex.
They will starve you of love,
they will leave your heart messy,
they will never offer you intimacy.
Love can only be offered from someone
looking for it,
not one looking for a mother or a maid.

When her smile starts to leave,
you are no longer competing for her heart
but with time.

You are not undeserving of love, grace, or
kindness even though people who were
undeserving of you prophesied this myth
over you.

Keep your ear away from their blasphemy.

Roses without thorns are just pretty plants.
Plants with thorns, yet without roses, are
just cactuses.
People without stories, scars, and a past
are not people.

Sometimes, it's not until what was
supposed to find you walks into your life
that you realize the blessing in those who
left.

Rivers won't flow from your eyes forever;
your heart will not always know a drought.
The wind will not always violently shake
you as it scans your soul.
The night eventually gives its shift to the
day, just as the moon surrenders its duty to
the sun.
Nothing stays the same,
not your pain, not your sadness,
not your bad days, not your mistakes.
Be hopeful.

When she is standing in her truth,
stand with her,
or choose to just stand behind her as she
comfortably marches deeper into it.

She is a woman first;
keep this truth alive in your mind.
Let it marinate in your heart and grow
roots within you.
She may be a wife carrying a love for you
that you never thought you'd be able to
believe in,
or a girlfriend you will never be able to
replace, a mother who shows why women
are such miracles.
Just like the fathers, the boyfriends, the
husbands, with their chests out boldly say,
"I am a man before anything," she is a
woman first and don't you forget that.

There are women who are misunderstood
and those who are understood but
unaccepted.
Despite that, be you, my dear.

She's learning to taste her own softness
and not chase it down with the sour part of
her.
Unbelieving that she is a bittersweet soul
rather than a sweet soul who's been bitter
at times is hard work for people like her.

Despite what they say men shouldn't do,
let your softness and the sweet side of you
be served to her with your love.
It'll only help her be more accepting of
herself and more sweet to you.

This is how you lead.

Emotional intelligence is not just encouraging her to not be led by emotions, but you are also learning to no longer suppress your emotions when she needs you to be emotionally open as well.

The pain,
the hurt,
all that you have faced help define you, but
they don't own your definition.
You are more than what you've endured
and overcome.

She is no longer looking at love and hate
as blurred lines that kept her heart stuck in
the gray area.

How can you be enough for someone who
isn't enough for themselves?
Most people do not know what being
enough means, let alone what you being
enough should look like.

She's got her own back.
Falling into the wrong hands has taught
her unreliable hands are not safer than
a back that has been stabbed enough to
develop its own way to soften the blow.

Share those traumatic experiences,
express those fears,
point at those insecurities,
let the wounds breathe.
Love will not come in
when the door is closed.
Open, open, open
to those who are truly knocking.

So few women have met intimacy and the peak of pleasure. Yet, so many men claim to be love artists who have mastered the art of pleasing and perfected intimacy with every stroke.

The gap is too far to not have real conversations about this.

Talk to her about it, not your boys.

Dear,

Please let your truth fly and be willing to teach those who want to learn your truth as well.

She desires peace just like the men who
proudly express that they are looking for a
woman who will be their escape.
Peace in her home, in her mind, and
written on the pages of her love story is a
priority to her as well.
When you say you want a love that will not
bring more chaos into your life, know that
she is searching for the same thing.

Good, mature, and loving men aren't afraid
of you speaking your mind;
they are afraid of not knowing what is
on your mind and tiptoeing around your
silence.

Part of loving her is learning to make love
to her the way she feels loved,
the way she finds pleasure,
the way she likes to be intimate.
When you say she likes something, let it be
confirmed by her not just assumed by your
ignorance or ego.

Intimate moments need communication to
feel like love.

Friends don't just disappear,
they fight, they disagree, they cry, and
whatever else,
then make up.
They don't just walk out of your life for
any silly reason.

Your boundaries will repel the wrong
people, but on the other hand,
they will strengthen your relationships
with the right ones.

Over time, all she had was herself.
When they left her, she was the only
person who did right by her.

Eventually, she learned to cherish her own
love, own presence, own space, and found
no reason to ever settle anymore.

The love you are offering her must
compete with her own love for herself.

Please never forget that
you are responsible for your love,
your mistakes,
your time,
your failure,
your heart.
Do not only remember that
but also own this truth.

They don't need to see that you are
beautiful; you just have to know that you
are.
Whether they see it or not,
your eyes seeing the beauty is what makes
the difference.

At this stage, she's well prepared to live a happily ever after that involves no one romantically. Although she would court her own presence into her sunset, she would rather find someone who is willing to share each other's heart and endure all the way to the end.

Depression is a demon that she's learned to grow deaf to despite how loud he catcalls her.
He has found a crack to slip through her soul far too many times after her heart shattered.
A mistake she's not giving another second to breathe into her life anymore nor a door to let anyone plant the seed of opportunity.

You are not cursed,
neither are all men that bad.
The unfortunate thing is that many of
us run into too many unfortunate events
before we meet our blessing.
I know meeting the wrong men is
exhausting, but it's not your fault.

Your fear of rejection is keeping too many
good things from you.
Your fear of failure is robbing you of
opportunities.
Your fear of heartbreak is keeping you
from the true love you desire.
Kick fear to the side, queen,
it's taking too much from you.

A love rich of memories, smothered with understanding, marinated with effort and seasoned by faith is what her heart longs for and her soul looks to savor.

His charm and manipulation are now
unconvincing magic tricks; they are an
illusion of love that will not prosper.
They can't be mislabeled anymore but
recognized as attempts from broken men to
take her heart and mind captive.

Live your truth, queen.
This is where living begins.

She's done renting parts of her to lovers
who need her to feel whole.
It's clear to her that empty hearts will
never be able to give her the love she
needs.

Effort is her love language.

Having more options than her is not brag-
worthy.
How can it be when someone is giving you
their entire heart, and you only put out one
hand just to make sure the other is free to
catch another that presents itself.
Being fully invested and committed is the
real flex; she needs someone who she is
sure will do what it takes to stay.

You've mistaken her unwavering love for chains that will forever keep her shackled to your feet.

Don't be so naive; she only follows after love. Where love isn't present, she may linger but will eventually flee.

Hold yourself accountable when you are being less than the great woman that you are.
The way you ask poor men to leave their excuses is the way you should leave yours behind.

Keep growing, queen.

Her idea of love is simple.

Her heart is only hungry for someone who is committed.

And by committed, not just committed to staying but committed to working through all the things that need to happen to see the love flourish into something powerful and beautiful.

When they call your boundaries selfish, too
much, too serious, or too aggressive,
remind yourself of why you set them.
To keep people who do not know you to
the core from telling you how to live even
when you show them what's best for you.

She's known betrayal and the power of its
flame.
Rest assured that it will never be how she
burns the bridges between the two of you.

Intimacy comes from unbuttoning her
mind and undressing her soul.

She said, "No."
Unless you have met her heart
and know the tone of her mind,
her "no" should always mean "no."
How can it sound like a "yes" when you
have not heard enough "yeses" from her.
And even then, you are capable of
misinterpreting them.

The pressure to be who and what they want you to be is a sacrifice too risky to take anymore.

Maturity is sometimes surrendering to love
and becoming all that it asks of you.

You may be tired of being robbed of
second chances with women like her.
But understand, women like her are just as
tired of men messing up their first chances.

To ever offer her the love she deserves, you must consider it an honor to have her heart resting in your hands.

She's not just an open book,
She is an unfinished poem that will take
attention, comprehension, devoted time,
and a hunger to see the author's heart and
the beauty in her story.

Can't you see safety in her eyes?
The way she is swimming her way out of
her past
to come to the shores of love.
There's nothing more beautiful than this:
to let your love be the current that helps
her float deeper into love.

How can your heart ever see how much
better she gets with time when you aren't
giving her time?

Be present in her presence.

Her mind will show you how to make love
to her, and her body will teach you how to
do it right.

When she becomes your world, you will see what good men who put their woman first brag about, why they are more disciplined to keep their relationship alive, why they aren't afraid of love or what silly titles people call men who are too deeply in love.

She's not after a high-value man;
all she wants is for you to see how valuable
she is, how valuable love is, and how
valuable the good man in you is.

If your legs get too heavy to walk away
from one of those lifeless relationships once
again, remember, it will only get worse and
suck the life out of you.

You must abandon your abandonment
issue to ever drink from her heart.

The truth is she doesn't throw her words or feelings around loosely, so when heartfelt words come out of her mouth, they are truly blooming from her heart.
When she expresses her feelings, know that they are coming from the depth of her soul.
Consider them, receive them, and know it is an act of bravery after all that she has gone through.

She is more than a vessel for pleasure, just as you are more than a vessel for provision.

Please remember to never settle for a man
who would rather suffocate his feminine
side than give it the freedom to melt in
your hands.

The taste of freedom has found her lips as
she dwells in her singleness; contentment is
no longer a rope attached to those she
cannot seem to let go of.

The way your roots hold on to the ground
when the storm arrives,
the way your ground stays fertilized with
love.

You don't need to change because they
want you to. You only need to change
when it's time for the shedding.

Don't be satisfied with your tears only
being water; let them become what
quenches the thirst of the tree of wisdom
finding roots in your mind.

She's been promised pleasure before, the
type of pleasure that only pleases them,
the type of pleasure men have passed down
amongst themselves as best-kept secrets on
how to keep a woman from leaving —
secrets that never asked her about what
pleases her,
secrets that are just gossip,
secrets that even help good men finish first
and leave her without ever seeing the finish
line.

There will be women who pique your
interest.
But her? She will pull in your attention
and demand that your eyes swallow every
inch of her existence
without ever saying a word.

She wore her scars like she wore her
lipstick.
You could not only see red,
but boldness on the lips of a warrior.

If her beauty lures you faster than her
heart,
you are swimming in the shallow parts.
There is depth in her speech,
her personality, her character, and her
mind.
Those parts of her are worth far much
more than the captivating art that she is.
Drown in her existence.
Breathe in all that she is.

The way she wears her flaws makes her flawless.

There is love and there is obsession.
Be both in love and obsessed with her.
Be obsessively in love with her.

The love like the one she has to offer
will breathe life into you in a way your
existence hasn't known.

If you cannot see the burden women like her carry, it is because you're the one loading her back.

She has lost interest in small talks, empty
conversations with men who put nice
questions as fill-ins so they can quickly
jump to asking questions toward sex.
You'll find out how freaky she is when you
know who she is deeply.
Know the game first before you start
counting bases.

There is love in her.
Some of it can easily be seen,
and some of it must be discovered.

The beauty their eyes see
is only a quarter of
how beautiful she really is;
yet, it's still captivating and mesmerizing.
It is like opening your eyes
for the first time
and seeing an angel.

Let her be your heaven on this earth.
It's the only way you'll see how God is a
mastermind.

In the mountains somewhere quiet,
where silence can silence her
thoughts and peace is thick in the air,
a place where she can hear herself
breathe and admire the simplicity of life.
That's where she needs to be.

Keep your dreams in front of you, dear.
Let your goals never fall from your priority
list.
Any man tying you down
isn't looking to keep you around to be his
life partner.
Who doesn't want to see someone they love
reach their peak?
How can good relationships be built on
teamwork, yet your partner doesn't want to
see his teammate thrive?

Listen to her heart.
It will give you the truth.
Believe her heart
more than you trust her lips.

Quit rewarding their inconsistency
when it's clear that choosing to not pour
the effort needed to build something special
is all they will be consistent at.

Show that you recognize her effort,
compliment her strength,
acknowledge her sacrifices,
celebrate her progresses.
Make her feel seen and she knows that you
have eyes for her heart.

Of course, there are feelings she doesn't
know how to express, words she has not
found a way to craft together to describe
many of her emotions, but there are things
she is certain about.
Listen to those things, give your attention
to them, build upon them, and it will
strengthen your connection with her.

I think you are beautiful just as you are.
I don't care if you disagree.
I don't care if anyone told you otherwise.
It's evident.
There is a glow about you,
a strength behind your smile,
and a confidence that flows through you
that is undeniable.
You don't have to believe anything I say,
except when I say that you are a beautiful
human.

Dear,

The more you hide and swallow your truth
to not hurt his ego, the more you are
hurting yourself and feeding his ego the
wrong things.
How you say things matter, but unspoken
things give too much room for
interpretation.
Saying them and learning how to say them
better is far more productive than not
saying them at all.

She did not change.
She grew while you expected
her to stay trapped inside
that old version of herself.

Only the selfish and the foolish
will find it hard to love you.
I am not saying this because
you are perfect or a saint
but because you're worth more than
they can understand, even with your flaws.
As you realize your worth,
you will also realize that
not too many people are
worth your time.

Do not try to lead her until
you are capable of leading
yourself and willing to
serve as well as follow.

Her effortless giggles,
her easily awakened laugh,
her openness are hints that she has
unlocked the door to her heart for you.
You are funnier, smarter, and listened to
more deeply when she has found a safe
place in you.
Come into her heart, but do not come in to
leave a mess.

You must learn to give her
reasons to be with you
without telling her why.

Her face,
her laugh,
her personality,
her existence can make an atheist
swear angels exist.

She cannot quickly fade out
of the memory of any man who
loved even the tiniest piece of her.
To taste a small fraction of her
is to invite a new addiction in.
Women like her live in the minds of
men in her past long after she has left.

Eventually,
your absence will lead them to regret.
By then, you won't need them to regret, to feel
sorry, or to be anything but gone out of your
life.

You cannot stop a woman like her
from being great.
Either you contribute to her
or gift her presence with your absence.

I know, dear, it's unfortunate.
They should see you as more than
a means to soothe their egos.
I cannot tell you you'll never
bump into any more of them.
I can only remind you that they do not
represent all men who walk on this earth.

Do not mistake her welcoming smile
for an invite, nor her niceness for flirtation.
Just because she treats you as human
beings should treat one another doesn't
mean she wants you.

Look at the way she conquers the darker
days in her life, like the moon piercing
through the night sky.
How could you not admire such resilience?

She has faced death to give life,
and that's how she learned not to give life
to what is dead.
She has far much more to live for than
love.

You are not missing out when you know
what you deserve and are unwilling to
open your heart until you or something
comparable is given to you.

She will not fall for your petty lies,
beautiful gestures, and trickery you use to
weaponize her desires to hold your spot in
her life.
How can you find nothing wrong with
using everything that looks like love to
walk over someone who only wants to love
you?

Loneliness will not trap her back into your snares.
She is learning to accept her own presence and growing in the understanding that the absence of a partner isn't the absence of love.

Her trust is in God, not man.

Her trust for men will only be led by God.

Your behavior will decide whether you
stay in her life; it will not be your words,
your potential, your intent, or anything
that is not clear, consistent, and true.

Let her speak.

Let her opinions fly freely.

Help her get comfortable with sharing her
opposite opinions.

Let the disagreement lead to good
conversations rather than conflict.

Give her voice room to grow and find its
tone.

Sloppy goodbyes aren't worth it.
Letting your silence speak for your absence
is sometimes the best exit plan.

Feeling everything is a blessing in itself, though it may feel like a curse, but being numb is too close to death to settle for feeling nothing at all.

Learn to use your words,
to form them without the emotions swelling
them up,
to let them exit your mouth.
Being logical isn't a "man thing."
It should also be a woman's thing.

A man who listens isn't the same as one who listens to reply.
If he's not looking to solve the issues together with you, everything you say will always be a problem.

She wants to get to know you—her eyes are dying to see your vulnerability, her hands aching to feel the softness of your heart, her ears dying to hear about the things that hurt you—and the things that make you feel alive.

As you search for the type of man a woman
like you needs, don't forget to keep
working on being the woman a man like
that also needs.

They'll keep pointing at your past choices
to prove a point.
Let them.
You just have to make sure you are using
the experience to build a better you.

When she becomes your world, you will
see how joyfully the stars dance in her
eyes.

Love is not a sport she will compete for,
nor is it a tennis match played with beating
hearts.

She's busy learning to love her image; you can keep dropping your likes under all the "baddies" pictures.

The answer is she will not let herself fall
into good things too quickly.
She's staying clear of making sacrifices too
fast, choosing to not dive heartfirst.
Her favorite place is slow with caution
now.
She's letting the memories create the
boundaries, the lessons give her wisdom.
She is verifying everything and listening to
her intuition more.
The only green light she is waiting for to
pour her heart into your hand is the red
flags to start fading out.

Intimacy needs communication to feel like love, just like it needs consent to feel right.

Pain may create a bond, but it doesn't help
most relationships find healing.
Broken people depending on love to make
them whole often break more hearts than
they love on.

Don't let them taking your softness for granted make you harder.

You will not be the heart she consumes
because of her cravings; you are not her
long-lost desire.
If she is asking for your heart, it's because
she wants to care for it and make a home
out of it.

She will not use her body as
she's grown to understand physical love
doesn't automatically translate to a love
that goes beyond just physical.

Spoil her with loyalty.
Feed her with truth.
Drink from the fountain of her love, and
never forget that it'll run dry without
consistency.

Feed her ears honesty, her eyes loyalty,
and drown her heart in consistency.

There are men who come to get what they
want and leave.
There are men who you're all they want
and one that will choose to never leave.

Your consistent presence is one of the most
beautiful ways to provide for her heart.

Learning to keep the pain at bay, away, in the past, has been the thing she practices the most.

Dear,

I pray the cloud of your mistakes doesn't
hang over you.
I pray the bad that has visited you doesn't
find a home in you.
I hope you don't let yesterday take all the
good of today from you.

You are not your mistakes.

I know the loss of that baby has grown an empty space in you, a hole that seems impossible to fill, a love that seems to have gone.

The grieving may never stop, the healing journey may never become complete, but please don't carry the guilt, don't carry the shame, don't let it break you.

Cold cannot be the temperature of your
heart or the temperature of your words.
Cold shoulders only carry bigger problems.

She has wasted too much on where there's
lack.
Therefore, she is not looking for a project
to fix, she's looking for someone who will
be equipped with what she's missed out on.

Maybe it's not accountability that she is afraid of; maybe she's refusing to flow with your demands and misguided expectations.

And sometimes what you want the most is
what you see everywhere.
Don't let love stories you do not know the
backstory of cause you to rush yours.

Drown out the noise that says your
standard is too much and that your needs
won't be met.

And sometimes the best way to draw out
the betrayal is to let it all burn through
you.

She understands you're busy, but busy
people always find a way to prioritize the
things that are most important to them.
Busy is never the problem, too busy for
love is what she doesn't like.

Isn't it strange that when they cheat on you, they try to poke at your weaknesses to cover up their own? Constantly scraping to find a soft spot in you that will surrender to the lie you've summoned this betrayal, that it's your fault they couldn't help themselves and have shown such a strong misrepresentation of love.

She'll be the first to tell you that there are
things she's enduring and growing out of
like coping mechanisms.

Dear,

I want you to know there are men who will
protect you whenever they see a wolf
preying on you.
Men who are not blind to disrespect, men
who will stand trying to stand out to you.
There are men who are tired of other men
treating you as less than sex.
I pray you run into those men more often.

Her slowly closing to you is giving you a chance to do what it takes to reopen the door or to at least put your foot against it and pause to talk about how you keep it from closing.

Sometimes the argument is the best sign of knowing she is fighting for the love story.

Whisper your secrets into her ears if you must; it's better than hearing it loudly and clearly from another mouth.

Learn to stop searching for love where it
isn't present.

She's both the beauty and the beast,
narrating her own fairy tale.

Perhaps her father showed her what love ought to be, yet the false lovers are the ones who muddied the water for her.

There are some who will enter your life to remind you why you should have a lock on the door of your heart and others to remind you that the door isn't meant to stay shut and locked for everyone.

She's choosing healing over numbness.

And as she loves you like no one else, love
her back like you've never loved anyone
else.

Having a man is not what makes you feel
all woman; his presence just amplifies it.

She knows that being completely
independent isn't healthy, but how can she
continue to run away from that idea when
men keep running from the role of
manhood with her.
Let's face it, her idea of not wanting a man
may have been inspired by her mother, but
the males she has met that were far from
men contributed greatly.

Being nice is not a weakness and being
mean isn't a superpower.
I'm sorry foolish men made you believe
this.

You'll always be needy looking into the
eyes of someone who doesn't need you.

The man for you will praise your femininity.

She'll feed you her heart in pieces because
enough men came in pretense and left once
she became all-in.

Depleted she became
after she gave and gave.

You like your women on the edge, strong
and no push back, unable to manipulate.
She likes her men empty of manipulative
tactics, purehearted, and emotionally
available.

The myths are debunked, the lies can no
longer hold her back from the truth.
She will no longer be obsessed with
someone else's approval simply because
that's what society has painted over her
mirror over and over again.

Fools are the men who treat her as if
leaving her youth is a curse, like the more
she ages, the more value she loses.
The more kids she has, the less desirable
she becomes.
What fool made up those silly ideas while
holding on to the fact that they are
desirable to younger women as older men,
dads swimming in dad bodies.

You're full of games, yet you don't like
when she plays by her own rules.

Dear,

You don't have to overcompensate for love
to compensate you.

Choose whether you want to be a friend or a lover. Complaining about the curse of being friends first when the intents are clear is creating an invisible zone where friends are trapped.

Can we just be friends, bosses, managers, and other things to women without trying to find a reward in just being with a woman?

When you say men and women can't be
friends, you're also saying you can't see
women as more than lovers and sex
partners.

As for her, she has no problem submitting;
she will submit to you as long as you're
submitting too.
She'll submit to you as long as you are
submitting to proper love, healthy
consistency, proper care of her heart.

Her heart recognizes you for
the good man that you are,
but it is her brain that
is consistently being worked on and
her soul that needs reassurance and
consistent evidence.

The reality is that some men will chase
after you because you are challenging.
They will ask for your number because it's
a number game to them.
They will carry conversations to loopholes
in your words.
They will do everything to win your heart
just to have it as a trophy.
The reality is some men never outgrow
their boyish outlook of love and never will.

The truth is, she isn't looking for much,
she is simply looking for love.
A love that isn't complicated, that isn't full
of excuses, that doesn't find itself making
the same promises over and over.
A love that doesn't come with constant
pain and uses lies to cover up its wrong.
She is looking for a love that looks like
love, for a man who acts like one, and for
a life where relationship doesn't drain it of
joy, peace, happiness.

The truth is, she isn't looking for much but
something real.

The end

Message to the reader:

Dear woman,
I hope HER has inspired you to find you,
brought confirmation to you, and helped
you see you in the right light, and that
you've continued to be you while growing
into better versions of you.
This book and every book in this series was
meant to help you process your thoughts,
feelings, and emotions, and remind you
that you aren't alone. It was also created to
remind you that your standards aren't too
high, you aren't demanding too much, and
that the wrong man will always make
excuses as to why he can't love you. I
penned all these words because, in an ugly
dating pool, it's easy to forget who you are,
what you bring to the table, and even what
love ought to look like.

I pray you revisit this book, that you discover the volumes that came before it, and always find the right message for the right moment in them. I started this series to tell men about the great things about HER I've observed and that they are overlooking and was surprised that it became a self-reminder to many women. I want to say thank you for reading, thank you for all the pages you've shared on your social media, and thank you for allowing my words to enter your hearts and your souls.

Dear man,

I commend you for coming on this journey and for choosing to take your time to learn more about HER. Too many men need to hear some of these things that they normally don't hear. Take these nuggets and see how they fit in your life. When you find HER, she will appreciate that you cared enough to consume these words. Men like you are the men your HER is looking for. I wrote these words to you too.

Acknowledgments

To Natalie, thank you for being my inspiration, my HER. The way you love me and teach me to love is the ink to my pen.

To my daughters, I love you dearly and hope these words can inspire even you.

To my son, I love you, and let these words be lessons to you as well. When you find her, become the HIM she needs you to be.

To everyone involved in this journey, thank you so much.

To you, the readers, your support means the world to me. Thank you for allowing my art to connect with your heART.

Other books by
Pierre Alex Jeanty

HER
HER Vol. 2
HIM
Ashes of Her Love
Sparking Her Own Flame
To the Women I Once Loved
Apologies That Never Came
Loving Me Right
In love with you
Heal Grow Love
Unspoken Feelings of a Gentleman
Unspoken Feelings of a Gentleman II
Watering Your Soil

Andrews McMeel Publishing
a division of Andrews McMeel Universal
1130 Walnut Street, Kansas City, Missouri 64106

www.andrewsmcmeel.com

23 24 25 26 27 MCN 10 9 8 7 6 5 4 3 2 1

ISBN: 978-1-5248-8064-4

Library of Congress Control Number: 2022949751

Illustrations by TreManda Pewett

Editor: Patty Rice
Art Director/Designer: Julie Barnes
Production Editor: Dave Shaw
Production Manager: Shona Burns